Puffin Books

THE HOUSE THAT CAUGHT A COLD

This is a delightful and inventive collection of poems from Richard Edwards. Read about the lazy genie who gets enough work for a lifetime, giggle at the naughty angel and wonder about UFOs – as Desmond did. There are also more serious poems such as Stevie Scared the bully, the nameless man, and the diner who is haunted by the starving African. Full of wit and humour with a wide variety of form, rhyme and rhythm, this is a collection to excite and enthral children for hours.

Richard Edwards was born in Kent in 1949 and educated at Sevenoaks School and the University of Warwick. In 1971 he won the Eric Gregory Poetry Award for an unpublished collection of poems.

By the same author

IF ONLY . . .
A MOUSE IN MY ROOF
WHISPERS FROM A WARDROBE
THE WORD PARTY

The House That Caught a Cold

Poems by Richard Edwards

Illustrated by Sarah Jane Stewart

PUFFIN BOOKS

PUFFIN BOOKS

Published by the Penguin Group
Penguin Books Ltd, 27 Wrights Lane, London W8 5TZ, England
Penguin Books USA Inc., 375 Hudson Street, New York, New York 10014, USA
Penguin Books Australia Ltd, Ringwood, Victoria, Australia
Penguin Books Canada Ltd, 10 Alcorn Avenue, Toronto, Ontario, Canada M4V 3B2
Penguin Books (NZ) Ltd, 182–190 Wairau Road, Auckland 10, New Zealand

Penguin Books Ltd, Registered Offices: Harmondsworth, Middlesex, England

First published by Viking 1991
Published in Puffin Books 1993
10 9 8 7 6 5 4 3 2 1

Printed in England by Clays Ltd, St Ives plc
Filmset in Plantin

Contents

The House That Caught a Cold

It ached. It groaned. It sniffed and coughed.
It shivered from its cellar to the rafters in its loft.

Its windows watered. Its doorbell wheezed.
It shattered all the china in its cupboards when it
  sneezed.

Its stair-treads creaked. Its pipes began to knock.
The hour hand wobbled wearily around its kitchen
  clock.

Its doors jammed stiff, their hinges needed oiling.
Its temperature went up so high the hot tank started
  boiling.

Along came the doctor: 'You do look ill.
Open up your letter-box and take this orange pill.'

The letter-box opened, the pill popped in,
The house gave a sigh, the house gave a grin,

The house cooled down and danced a little dance
And feeling quite recovered went on holiday to France

Where, strolling on the promenade, with winking stars
  above,
It met a pretty villa with a porch and fell in love,

They honeymooned in Normandy and now, outside
  Calais,
Live quietly side by side – with an extension on the
  way.

Waterway Robbery

A pike in the river
Had cornered a carp:
'Five pounds or your life
And you'd better look sharp!'
The carp gasped and bubbled:
'Five pounds! But I'm clean,
I don't carry money,
I haven't a bean.'
The pike grinned: 'No matter,

They say carp's quite tasty.'
'Oh, give me a chance,'
Begged the carp, 'don't be hasty;
Just wait here one minute
And, quick as a flash,
I'll go and come back
With the relevant cash.'
'OK,' hissed the pike.
'One minute you've got
To pay me before
Things start getting hot.
Now scram!' The carp did
And as fast as you like
Returned with a fiver
To pay off the pike
Who left with a swirl
Of his emerald flanks, . . .
'Thank goodness,' the carp thought,
'That rivers have banks!'

One Wet Day

Jackie put her red shoes on
And her red coat
And her red woolly hat
And went out of the back door into the garden
To pick a strawberry.

Jimmy put his green boots on
And his green coat
And his green woolly hat
And went out of the back door into the garden
To cut a lettuce.

Zuleika put one black and one orange shoe on
And her gold sash,
Stuck a feather in her hair
And went out of the back door into the rain forest
To track panthers.

The Vault of Unwanted Inventions

The Vault of Unwanted Inventions
Is a sad and a funny old place,
Where the self-raising hat that has never been worn
Waits locked in its ebony case,
Where the yodelling scarecrow for farmers
And the pair of soundproof pyjamas,
The paint-spraying lamp-post for scaring off dogs,
The seven-houred clock and the litter-spike clogs
Lie patiently gathering dust,
Or slowly beginning to rust.

The Vault of Unwanted Inventions
Is a sad and a funny old room,
Where Moffat's magnetic suspenders for socks
Shine mournfully out of the gloom,
Where the plate with no bottom for slimmers
And the buoyant false teeth for non-swimmers,
The head-rest for roses beginning to droop,
The rhubarb detector, the scarf for cold soup,
The ant-bath, the sneezer, the four-legged tight,
The portable moon for a very dark night
And other things equally clever
Will probably languish for ever,
Preserved, with the best of intentions,
In the Vault of Unwanted Inventions.

The Snake

I hate the snake
I hate the snake
I hate the way it trails and writhes
And slithers on its belly in the dirty dirt and creeps
I hate the snake
I hate its beady eye that never sleeps.

I love the snake
I love the snake
I love the way it pours and glides
And esses through the desert and loops necklaces
   on trees
I love the snake
Its zigs and zags, its ins and outs, its ease.

I hate the snake
I hate the snake
I hate its flickering liquorice tongue
Its hide and sneak, its hissiness, its picnic-wrecking spite
I hate its yawn
Its needle fangs, their glitter and their bite.

I love the snake
I love the snake
I love its coiled elastic names
Just listen to them: hamadryad, bandy-bandy,
   ladder,
Sidewinder, asp
And moccasin and fer de lance and adder

And cascabel
And copperhead
Green mamba, coachwhip, indigo –
So keep your fluffy kittens and your puppy-dogs,
    I'll take
The boomslang and
The anaconda. Oh, I love the snake!

Tall Paul

When I was small, they'd smile and say:
'Don't worry, Paul, that's just the way
You're built; you'll grow up tall one day.'

But now I'm grown and *seven feet* tall,
They smile and say: 'Don't worry, Paul,
Er . . . have you thought of basketball?'

Thirteen Witches and Three Chants

It's dark tonight
The moon's in hiding
Over the roof-tops
Witches are riding
Each on a broomstick
Each with a cat
Each with her name
On the brim of her hat.

Old Malavita,
Young Villanelle,
Quinch,
Pantucket,
Guzzle,
Fell,
Wixa,
Tapfoot,
Greenthumb,
Sly,
Itchwitch,
Kitchenwitch,
Venom with the Eye.

Come to the window
Stand and stare
Thirteen witches
Swishing through the air
Thirteen witches
Riding out of sight
Doing witch business
On All Souls' Night.

Wixa,
Tapfoot,
Venom with the Eye,
Itchwitch,
Kitchenwitch,
Greenthumb,
Sly,
Quinch,
Pantucket,
Guzzle,
Fell,
Old Malavita,
Young Villanelle.

I Guzzle's Chant

Buckets of fat
Cream for the cat
Wriggly spaghetti for lunch
Syrup and spice
Crystallized mice
Crisp crinkly crackling to crunch.

Plums from the tree
Eels from the sea
Puddings that steam on the spoon
Chickens, noodling
Apples, strudeling
Cheese from the tub of the moon.

Honey and ham
Spread, scoop and cram
Slump on the table and snore
Dream of fried fishes
Sizzling on dishes
Wake and guzz-guzzle some more.

Blankets of tripe
Pears leaky-ripe
Rubbery rashers to chew
Junket and juice
Jellified goose
Sausage salami and stew!

II Venom's Chant

Mine's a bad eye
When I wake
Hooligans' knees go
Quake quake quake
Mine's a bad eye
When I glare
Boots lose laces
Heads lose hair.

Mine's a bad eye
When I peek
Big-heads blubber
Show-offs shriek
Mine's a bad eye
When I glower
Cheese turns rancid
Milk turns sour.

Mine's a bad eye
When I frown
Bullies' trousers
Slide right down
Louts grow pimples
Boasters shrink
Mine's a bad eye
Wink, wink, wink!

III Tapfoot's Chant

Willow by the water
Weeping tree
Be uprooted, dance like me.

Statue in the dreaming
Midnight park
Kick your heels up, dance in the dark.

Signpost at the crossroads
Scarecrow by the corn
Swing those arms and dance till dawn.

Cooker in the kitchen
Hatstand in the hall
Dummy in the dress-shop, ladder by the wall
Kitten in the garden
Spider on the sill
Stoat in the undergrowth, rabbit on the hill
Lobster in the rockpool
Starfish in the sea
Dance like Tapfoot, dance like me.

Ladders

Beep! from the street – a rusty van,
Standing beside it a tall thin man:
'Ladders!

Ladders wobbly, ladders steady,
Ladders for trees when plums are ready,
Ladders!

Ladders new, ladders old,
Ladders for painting ceilings gold,
Ladders!

Ladders narrow, ladders wide,
Ladders for lofts with ghosts inside,
Ladders!

Ladders short, ladders tall,
Ladders for scaling a palace wall,
Ladders!

Ladders for saving skaters who
Braved thin ice and plunged right through,
Ladders to take you out of Monday
Back into bed on a lazy Sunday,
Ladders!

Ladders silver, ladders brown,
Ladders for climbing out of town,
Up past chimneys, up so high,
Higher than clouds or an eagle's eye,
Till, five miles beneath your feet,
You see in a tiny winding street
The tiny figure of a tall thin man
Who stands and shouts by a rusty van:
Ladders!'

Across the Universe

A man in his yard looking up at the stars
Wondered – can there be life out there?
People like us with two hands and two feet
And a face and a body and hair?

A man in his yard looking up at the stars
From a different corner of space
Wondered – can there be people like us out there
With a body, hands, feet and a face?

Both men in both yards scratched the end of their
    chins,
Both shivered, both paused a short pause,
Said 'Probably not,' and went slowly inside,
Both closing identical doors.

Groan!

The baker's making bread,
His brow is hot and beaded,
The pummelled dough
Is happy though –
It's so nice to be kneaded.

The Uninvited Guest

I like to chew a chewy chop,
I like to load my fork
With steak, with rich brown casserole,
With chunks of veal and pork.

I like my sweet, I like my cheese,
I like my splosh of wine,
I like to spread and guzzle when
I settle down to dine.

Eating's my only hobby, friend,
My passion and delight,
So that's why I was so put out
At dinner-time last night,

For as I sliced my Parma ham,
Luminously thin,
I looked up from my plate to see
Some fellow staring in.

His face was black as Africa,
His arms were skin and bone,
His ribs protruded through his chest
Like keys of a xylophone,

And, worst of all, the blighter had
No clothes on – starkers, nude!
Enough to put a decent chap like me
Right off his food.

The police, I thought, they'll see to him,
I got up from my chair
And, sure as eggs is scrambled eggs,
He vanished into air!

Shaken? I should say. It doesn't
Happen every day
That some bare savage eyes you up,
Then disappears away.

His face was black as Africa,
His arms were sticks, so thin
You'd think they'd break just moving,
No flesh, just bones and skin . . .

But, as they say, life trundles on.
What's that? Dessert, old man?
I'll say. Just when have I refused
A piece of cherry flan?

So scoop the trifle squelchy deep
And pile the whipped cream high.
Africa? Where's Africa?
Waiter! Bring more pie!

Weather Lane

As I walked out one morning,
Walking down Weather Lane,
I met a man all dressed in grey,
His name was Mr Rain,
He wore a hat of drizzle
That dripped down on his nose
And squelch, squelch, squelch inside
His sloppy gumboots went his toes.

As I walked out one afternoon,
Walking my small dog, Joe,
I met a man all dressed in white,
His name was Mr Snow,
He wore a coat of crystals
And as he moved along
The icicles that fringed his beard
Went cling and clang and clong.

As I walked out one evening,
With daylight almost done,
I met a man all dressed in gold,
His name was Mr Sun,
He wore a shining buckle
And as he passed me by
Went sizzle, sizzle, sizzle
Like a sausage on to fry.

As I walked out one midnight,
Hurrying to keep warm,
I met a man all dressed in black,
His name was Mr Storm,
And when he'd blustered by me
He veered around and said,
'You're out too late,' went huff puff puff
And blew me back to bed.

Daniel and the Lions

The six lions
On the lampshade
In Daniel's midnight room,
Wake up when Daniel's fast asleep
And blink in the gloom,
And shake their manes
And yawn and leap down
Softly to the floor,
Free, as long as darkness lasts,
To prowl round and explore.

Imagine them:
One hunts a spider
Through the carpet pile,
One springs on to the windowsill
To moonbathe for a while,
The others, round
The bedlegs run
Miniature lion races,
But all six jump back up at dawn
To take their usual places
And welcome Daniel
Back from sleep
With the familiar sight
Of six lions on a painted lampshade –
Longing for the night.

I Gave My Love a Red Red Nose

I gave my love a red red nose
By accident. You see,
While sniffing at the red red rose,
She woke a sleeping bee.

The Birdwatcher's First Notebook

Monday – to the reservoir,
Real beginner's luck,
Saw a quack-quack-quacking thing,
Think it was a . . . grebe.

Tuesday – to the farmyard,
Only mud, but then
Saw a cluck-cluck-clucking thing,
Think it was a . . . partridge.

Wednesday – out at midnight,
Tom-cats on the prowl,
Heard a twit-twit-twooing thing,
Think it was a . . . nightingale.

Thursday – to the seaside,
Weather grey and dull,
Saw a big white wailing thing,
Think it was a . . . spoonbill.

Friday – brown bird on the lawn,
Outside in a rush,
Saw a worm tug-tugging thing,
Think it was a . . . pipit.

Saturday – to the heathery moor,
Scanned the sky and hark!
Heard a trill-trill-trilling thing,
Think it was a . . . curlew.

Sunday – tired of birdwatching,
Made a bamboo wicket,
Asked some friends round, cadged a bat,
Had a game of . . . football.

Oh, Ozzie!

'Polar bear in the garden!' yelled Ozzie,
And we all rushed out to see,
But of course it wasn't a bear at all –
Just a marmalade cat who'd jumped over the wall.
Oh, Ozzie!

'Mountain lion in the garden!' yelled Ozzie,
And we all rushed out to see,
But of course it wasn't a lion with a roar –
Just the scruffy black dog who'd dug in from next door.
Oh, Ozzie!

'Kangaroo in the garden!' yelled Ozzie,
And we all stayed in and smiled,
And of course it wasn't a kangaroo –
But a man-eating tiger escaped from the zoo.
Poor Ozzie.

Lower the Diver

Lower the diver over the side
Down to the roots of the swirling tide.

Lower the diver, weighted with lead,
Glass and brass helmet over his head.

Lower the diver on to the deck
And the barnacled masts of the long-lost wreck.

Lower the diver; will he find jars,
Rust-sealed treasure-chests, silver bars?

Lower the diver; will he find gold,
Cannon-balls, skulls, or an empty hold?

Lower the diver; pray that the shark
Doesn't mind guests in the salty dark.

Lower the diver; then man the winch,
Wind him up slowly, inch by inch.

Undo his helmet. Why does he weep?
Is it so bad to be hauled from the deep?

Talk to the diver. What does he mean –
'Mermaids are real and her eyes were green'?

Fred Firth

Fred Firth saw a little bird
Flying from a wall,
'Ah!' said Fred. 'It must be wings
That don't let birdies fall.'

Fred Firth built himself some wings,
Climbed up on a chair,
Closed his eyes and with one flap
Jumped into the air.

Fred Firth nosedived to the floor,
Crashed and bumped his head.
'Ah!' said Fred. 'It can't be wings –
Must be beaks instead.'

Out of the Night

You dance by dusky water,
You haunt along the stream,
You wait until the bat squeaks from the sky,
You slip in through my window
As softly as a dream,
You stealthily approach me where I lie;

You're delicate and dainty,
Your song, though faint, is fine,
Your limbs are long and very slender too,
Your touch, at first, is gentle
But, really, must you dine
On me, mosquito? I would not on you.

The Lazy Genie

An old lamp in the attic –
Snores coming from its spout –
Marie gave it a shake – a lazy
Genie tumbled out.

'Three wishes I must grant you,'
Yawned the genie to Marie,
'So wish away, it's your reward
For liberating me.'

'Well, first I'd like a toffee,'
Marie quietly replied,
'And second, a fat doughnut
With a blob of jam inside.'

That's lucky, thought the genie,
This girl is easily pleased,
'And what's your third and final wish –
A gobstopper?' he teased.

'My third and final wish? I think
I know what that'll be –
To have ten million million wishes more,
Please,' said Marie.

Three of a Kind

I stalk the timberland,
I wreck and splinter through,
I smash log cabins,
I wrestle grizzly bears.
At lunch-time if I'm dry
I drain a lake or two,
I send the wolves and wolverines
Howling to their lairs.
I'm Sasquatch,
Bigfoot,
Call me what you like,
But if you're a backpacker
On a forest hike,
Keep a watch behind you,
I'm there, though rarely seen.
I'm Bigfoot,
Sasquatch,
I'm mean, mean, mean.

I pad across the snow field,
Silent as a thief,
The phantom of the blizzard,
Vanishy, rare.
I haunt the barren glacier
And men in disbelief
Goggle at the footprints
I scatter here and there.
I'm Abominable,
Yeti,
Call me what you choose,

But if you're a mountaineer,
Careful when you snooze,
I'm the restless roaming spirit
Of the Himalayan Range.
I'm Yeti,
Abominable,
I'm strange, strange, strange.

I rear up from the waves,
I thresh, I wallow,
My seven snaky humps
Leave an eerie wake.
I crunch the silly salmon,
Twenty at one swallow,
I tease the silly snoopers –
A fiend? A fish? A fake?
I'm The Monster,
Nessie,
Call me what you please,
But if you're a camper
In the lochside trees,
Before you zip your tent at night
Say your prayers and kneel.
I'm Nessie,
The Monster,
I'm real, real, real.

Stevie Scared

Stevie Scared, scared of the dark,
Scared of rats, of dogs that bark,
Scared of his fat dad, scared of his mother,
Scared of his sis and his tattooed brother,
Scared of tall girls, scared of boys,
Scared of ghosts and sudden noise,
Scared of spiders, scared of bees,
Scared of standing under trees,
Scared of shadows, scared of adders,
Scared of the devil, scared of ladders,
Scared of hailstones, scared of rain,
Scared of falling down the drain,
Stevie Scared, scared of showing
He's so scared and people knowing,
Spends his whole time kicking, fighting,
Shoving, pinching, butting, biting,
Bashing little kids about
(Just in case they find him out).

Last Words

'I fear the sun, I fear the sun,
The sun is not my friend,
The sun will be the death of me,
The sun will be my end.
If I had my way, we'd be ruled
For ever by the moon
And lovely freezing nights would not
Give way to dawn or noon,
But as it stands, it's you or me, sun,
One of us must go,'
The icicle said, weeping
From the bathroom overflow.

Don't Swat

Jane walked towards the first hive –
A fierce and furious sound
As hordes of spiteful bees swarmed out
And chased her round and round.

Jane walked towards the second hive –
Silence, not one wing,
Jane opened up the hive and saw
A very curious thing,

For there, sealed in the honey
And walled around with comb,
A shiny bracelet lay, inscribed
'DON'T TOUCH. LEAVE ME ALONE!'

Its gleam was a temptation
Too powerful to resist,
Jane took the sticky bracelet out
And clicked it on her wrist.

But, oh, she should have left it,
For, quick as you can blink,
The grass grew tall as little Jane
Began to shrink and shrink.

Her eyes bulged out, her body
And six legs fuzzed with fur,
The wings that opened on her back
Started to flap and whirr,

And off she went, buzz-buzzing
Unhappily to and fro,
With house and family left behind
Like little dots below.

So if, while in your garden,
Or near some orchard plot,
Or in the hills, or any other
Warm and nectary spot,

You see an insect looking
More human than most bees,
Just spare a thought – it might be Jane,
So don't swat, don't swat, please!

Samooreena

When Samooreena went away
Milk turned sour and grass turned grey,
Come home, Samooreena.

When Samooreena went away
Tortoises stayed in all day,
Poets couldn't find one rhyme,
Climbing roses didn't climb,
Come home, Samooreena.

When Samooreena went away
Garden hoses wouldn't play,
Birds, instead of singing, wailed,
Clocks ran down, the harvest failed,
Toast went soggy, soup got lumps,
Maude got measles, I got mumps,
Come home, Samooreena.

Now she's back! Oh, Samooreena,
Blades of grass were never greener,
Tortoises stretch out and run
Faster than rabbits in the sun,
Poets cry 'Ah! Spoon and June!'
Climbing roses brush the moon,
Hoses gush and spout and stream,
Toast's like crackling, soup's like cream,
Wheat's all ears, the milk tastes sweet,
Clocks go tick-tock, birds tweet-tweet,
Maude, unmeasled, skips, while I
Mumpless on my soapbox cry
'Samooreena, Samooreena,
Stay here, Samooreena!'

The Market

I went to the market and bought a fish
That swam in a small glass sea,
I looked at the fish and pouted,
The fish turned tail on me.

I went to the market and bought a bird
That perched on a small wire swing,
I looked at the bird and whistled,
The bird refused to sing.

I went to the market and bought a mouse
That ran in a small tin wheel,
I looked at the mouse and snuffled
And asked 'How do you feel?'

And the mouse squeaked back 'Much better than you,
For although I am not free,
I shall never buy a bird in a cage
Or a fish in a small glass sea.'

Dorothy Porridge

Dorothy Porridge is wearing a lettuce
And nobody quite knows why,
She's racing around like the spin of a coin
And shaking her fist at the sky,
The last time I saw her she lifted a leaf
And gave me a wink of her eye,
Dorothy Porridge is wearing a lettuce
And nobody quite knows why.

Captain Catt

With sharpened harpoon ready
Brave Captain Catt set sail,
Heading for the polar seas
To find and hunt the whale.

The waves were wild as horses
But Captain Catt was strong
And wrestling with the kicking wheel
He steered his ship along,

Until, one glittering morning
He reached Bloodblubber Bay,
Where every summer schools of whales
Gathered to feed and play.

The Captain climbed his mainmast
And scanned the sea for tails,
For fins, for wakes, for water spouts,
For any sign of whales.

'Come up, you cringing cowards!'
Cried Catt. 'I know you're there.
Come up and wave your fine flukes
In the cold and crystal air.'

A week passed by, a fortnight,
But still no whales would come,
The Captain stamped and swore and spat
And sulked and took to rum,

And swigged and cursed and guzzled
Until his bloodshot eyes
Made out, one bleary evening,
A ghostly whale-shape rise.

'At last,' he breathed. 'My beauty!
Now if I'm cool and quick,
I'll have you wallowing in blood,
You son of Moby Dick!'

He aimed, he flexed his shoulder
And hurled the harpoon high
Towards what was, the Captain thought,
The whale's shining eye.

But Captain Catt had blundered –
He'd launched his keen harpoon
Straight at a crusty crater in
The round and rising moon.

The barb hooked home, the Captain
Clung grimly to the rope . . .

. . . So if one night you're studying
The moon by telescope,

And see in lunar orbit
A tiny comet whiz,
A comet with a Captain's cap,
You'll know just who it is.

Brave Captain Catt goes wailing
Through cold space every night,
While down below all spouting whales
(And I) say 'Serves him right!'

The Dentures' Complaint

Ungrateful old codger, why, why, why,
When we help you smile so brightly
And let you eat radishes, rashers and roasts
Do you try to drown us nightly?

The Greenhouse

There's a smell of heat and jungle,
There's a smell of peat and loam
In the greenhouse,
There are trays and tubs and tubers,
There's a one-eared garden gnome
In the greenhouse,
There are little sounds of growing, you can hear the
    tiny shoots
Spreading out their new green wings, pushing down
    their wriggly roots,
You can hear a spider spinning round a pair of old
    brown boots
In the greenhouse.

When it's bitter in the garden
It is always dry and warm
In the greenhouse,
There's the perfect rainproof shelter
From a raging thunderstorm
In the greenhouse,
The downpour swats and rattles with a batter and a din
And the wild wind wails loudly like a crazy violin –
It can wail all it wants to, it won't find its cold way in
To the greenhouse.

When I'm old and grey and creaky
I shall sit and dream all day
In the greenhouse,
Watching clouds and sun and shadows,
Watching leaf-light glance and play
In the greenhouse,
Watching petals tumble slowly from a shaken yellow
    rose,
Watching young flowers as they open, watching old
    ones as they close,
Sinking deeper in my deckchair as I doze and doze and
    doze
In the greenhouse.

The Window

She looks in through the window
And wonders who they are —
The woman in the green silk dress,
The man with a cigar,
The black cat on the rocking-chair,
The girl in bows and lace,
The boy who sees her looking in
And pulls a funny face.

She steps back from the window
And rubs her eyes and blinks —
But no one's lived in this old house
For years and years, she thinks;
And when she looks again the room
Is dark and cold and bare,
Just brick-ends, shadows, spiders
And a broken rocking-chair.

The Doctor of Dreams

'Lie on that couch,' the doctor said, 'and tell me about
  your dreams,
Then listen to my explanation – nothing's what it
  seems.
You dream, I think, of saxophones, of stairways made
  of ice,
You dream of wading backwards through a sea of
  boiled rice.'

'Well, no . . .' I said. 'Aha!' the doctor cried. 'As I
  suspected,
You dream of robbing sausage shops and going
  undetected,
You dream of climbing Everest on yards of vanished
  rope
And getting to the top to find the mountain's made of
  soap.'

'It's not exactly that,' I said. 'I see,' the doctor hissed.
'You dream of joining dachshunds in a game of
  German whist,
You dream of wearing sticky shoes, of flying like a
  parrot,
Or else that if you're touched by rain you'll turn into a
  carrot.'

'Please stop!' I shouted, getting up and reaching for
    my coat.
'I only came to see you with a case of tickly throat.
I never dream of sausage shops, I never dream of rain,
And now, if you'll excuse me, I must hurry for my
    train.'

I left and from the corridor I heard the doctor mutter:
'A train! Of course! With oval wheels that run on
    tracks of butter.'
I shook my head and sighed, then spreading treacle on
    my feet,
Slid slowly down the melting stairs and flew into the
    street.

The Glove and the Guitar

A toy guitar
And an old green glove
Meeting on the rubbish dump
Fell in love.

'How smooth, how plump,
How curved you are,'
Said the old green glove
To the toy guitar.

Said the toy guitar,
'My dusty heart sings
When I think of your fingers
Tickling my strings.'

Dusk and darkness
And, oh, what a fright
The neighbourhood tom-cats
Got that night,

When they heard from the dump
Strange sounds coming,
Sounds of plucking,
Sounds of strumming,

Sounds of a wild
Flamenco tune,
As the glove and the toy guitar
Played beneath the moon.

Nameless

Where are you going, man in grey,
Shabby and sad on this bright blue day?

I'm looking for my name.

Why do you search along the gutter,
Poke through dustbins, moan and mutter?

I'm looking for my name.

Why do your fingers trace each mark
Carved on trees and benches in the park?

I'm looking for my name.

Why do you study trails in the grass,
The secret words of frost on glass?

I'm looking for my name.

Where are you going, man in grey,
Shaking your head as you walk away?

I'm looking for my name. I'm looking for my name.

Maria's Party

Maria has a friend who is a spider –
She keeps it in her satchel in a box,
Maria has a friend who is a beetle –
It scuttles in a drawer behind her socks,
Maria has a friend who is a grass snake –
It slithers in a suitcase in the shed,
Maria has a friend who is a big grey slug –
She hides it in a jar beneath her bed.
Last week Maria asked her mother sweetly:
'Next Friday, can I have some friends to tea?'
Her mother said: 'Of course. Let's have a party.
I'll make some special cakes; we'll start at three.'

Maria's little friends enjoyed the party.
The beetle built a cave from crumbs of food,
The grass snake chased the spider through a trifle,
The slug sat on a scone and slowly chewed.
Yes, everyone enjoyed Maria's party,
A triumph, surely no one could deny,
Except, perhaps, Maria's missing mother –
She's still locked in the toilet . . . wonder why?

Out of a Cloud

I have never seen one,
Desmond saw one though,
He said it hummed like hives of bees,
He said it glowed a glow,
He said it swooped out of a cloud
And lit the fields below,
He said it took his heart away,
Desmond's UFO.

Of course no one believed him,
But wandering here and there,
Desmond scanned the sky each night
With his hopeful stare,
Examining the Milky Way,
Venus, the Plough, the Bear,
Searching, wishing, longing,
Desmond head-in-air.

And then, one day, he vanished.
How? We'll never know.
We found no clue or trace of him,
Hunting high and low,
Just, spiked on to a barbed-wire fence,
A note saying 'Told you so,'
And all around the grass pressed down . . .
Where did Desmond go?

Cupboard Crush

'Tomato, why do you lie there,
Sighing such desperate sighs?
What's wrong?' asks the soft-hearted lettuce,
And the blushing tomato replies:
'I have fallen in love with King Edward –
Those eyes, those eyes, those eyes!'

Down in the Cellar

Don't go down the cellar steps,
Stay up in the hall,
People trying the creaky cellar staircase
Sometimes fall.

– But my friends are in the cellar,
The little bugs that run
On eight legs up my trouser ends
To have their ticklish fun.

– My friends are in the cellar,
The little ghosts that glide
Like blown smoke through the dusty dark
To nestle by my side.

– My friends are in the cellar,
The little rats that sneak
And nose their furry way into my shirt
And squeak, squeak, squeak.

– So you can stay here safely
And snugly in the hall,
But I'm going down the cellar stair
To meet my friends who live down there,
Who scamper, scratch and float through air
And scurry by the wall
And haunt and creep and crawl.

Walking Out

Bored with people telling her
Which clothes she ought to wear,
Which colours would be flattering,
Which way to cut her hair,

Bored with worrying how to lose
A sag, an inch, a stone,
She took her body off one day
And walked out in her bone.

It wasn't cold. The warm breeze buffed
Her spine until it shone,
She skipped a bit – how free it felt
To be a skeleton!

She crossed a field: friendly moos
From kind unstartled cattle,
They waved their tails, she waved her hands –
Rattle, rattle, rattle.

She crossed a wood: brambles raked
Her shins but did no harm,
A song-thrush and a lazy robin
Hitched lifts on her arm.

She crossed a bridge and stopped to watch
Her image on the river,
An eel wove between her ribs
Making her shadow shiver.

She reached the shore. Whispering waves
Ran up. Would they support her?
She crossed the sea, she crossed the sea:
Bone on the water.

Spare a Thought

Spare a thought for the front-door mat,
Scratching-pad of a mangy cat,
Mud-gunged, balding, full of holes,
Poked by high-heels, scraped by soles,
Worn, downtrodden, booted flat –
Spare a thought for the front-door mat.

Spare a thought for the hoover, please,
Gobbling grit and mongrel fleas,
Kicked by chair-legs, bruised by doors,
Choked by dust and fluffy floors –
No surprise its innards wheeze –
Spare a thought for the hoover, please.

Spare a thought for the bathroom soap,
Clawed and gouged by clumsy grope,
Rubbed round armpits, dirty faces,
Feet and other nasty places,
Life for soap's a slippery slope –
Spare a thought for the bathroom soap.

Spare a thought for all punished things –
Trampolines and wrestling rings,
Nails being hammered, gongs being bashed,
Eggs being beaten, spuds being mashed,
Dartboards, drums and sofa springs,
Oh, spare a thought for punished things!

On Looking into the Grand Canyon

The Colorado chuckles –
Me, I'd laugh,
Knowing I was strong enough
To slice the world in half.

The Angel

She looked over her shoulder –
Nobody was near,
The clouds seemed deserted,
The coast seemed clear,
So the angel up in heaven
Undid her shining wings
And shrugged them off: nasty
Heavy old things.

She leapt – she vaulted –
Cartwheeled – somersaulted –
Back-flipped – landed –
Sprang – hand-standed –
Gyrated on her halo,
Legs up in the air,
Nightie round her shoulders,
Body all bare.

What was that? A noise,
Something like a cough,
And as no angel's decent
With her white wings off,
She zipped them back and, just in time,
Started praying fast
As, wrapped in all his mystery,
God strolled past.

Stowaway

Tarantula, tarantula,
Hidden in your crate,
Can you feel your hunger
Turning into hate?

Tarantula, tarantula,
Being swung ashore,
What are all those whiskers
And those fine fangs for?

Tarantula, tarantula,
Lowered to the quay,
Will you thank the greengrocer
When he sets you free?

Tarantula, tarantula,
Scuttling out of sight,
Whose bed will your darkness
Glide beneath tonight?

Longing

The small blue boat
Tugs on its rope,
Dying to be free,
While fins
And tins
And twigs
And sprigs
And tide
And glide
And eels
And keels
And whirls
And swirls
And sticks
And slicks
And litter
And glitter
And tails
And sails
And crates
And spates
And floats
And boats
And sweepings from the quay
Pass
Bobbing, prancing,
Ducking, dancing
Downstream to the sea.

Suddenly

Suddenly everything stopped:
The sparrow in mid-cheep
The spider in mid-spin
The kitten in mid-leap
The pony in mid-trot
The falcon in mid-glide
The rabbit in mid-nibble
The servant in mid-stride.

Suddenly everything stopped.
'You see,' old Merlin said,
'I still have certain powers,
Although confined to bed,
Although . . .' Then Merlin sighed,
His last breath almost gone,
Just time to snap his fingers –
And everything moved on.

Index of First Lines

Some more poetry in Puffin

THE BEST OF FRIENDS
Tony Bradman

A varied and humorous collection of poems which explore just what friendship means to a child. It includes verse from Kit Wright, Colin McNaughton, Roger McGough and many others and looks at many different types of friends in a lively and accessible way.

A HOUSE IN MY ROOF
Richard Edwards

A delicious collection of poetry for younger children which is funny, quirky and highly original. Richard Edwards brings his exceptional and individual wit and charm to an unexpected variety of subjects – even including 'The Thing Extraordinaire'! There are tales with unexpected twists, the strangest of conversations, and a mixture of reality and magic children will love.

SEA IN MY MIND
Selected poems from *The Observer* National Children's Poetry Competition

This collection of remarkable poetry by children covers a wide range of subjects from love and loss, to people and places, from birds and beasts, to wind and water. Chosen from top entries and award winners in *The Observer* National Children's Poetry Competition, this selection is an enlightening and enjoyable look at the world by young people today.